I'm Happy!

Building Self-Esteem in Children

Written by
Latrice Slaughter

Illustrated by
Ajaye Herndon

Published And Distributed By
Lioness Publishing
Email: livia.latrice@gmail.com

Packaging/Consulting
Lioness Publishing
Email: livia.latrice@gmail.com

Cover design: Ajaye Herndon
First printing September 2017
978-0-9961606-2-9
10987654321

Dedications

Lateace, I am grateful that I can call you my sister. Thank you for all that you do in helping me to achieve my goals. I love you always.

Amaiyah, even though you are in college now you will always be my little princess. Go all the way! Stay focused, stay driven, and continue to live life on your terms. Reach for the stars, princess! I love you always.

Ajaye' Herndon, thanks for helping me bring my vision to life. This book would not be a success without you. Thank you! You go boy!

And to the world, Be Happy!

Hi there! My name is Bree, my smile is so big, I am as happy as can be!

"I am a happy little girl!" I tell myself this everyday. I feel good about who I am in every single way!

"I am Happy! I am Happy!"
I say it all the time!
Sometimes I say it loud.....

...or quietly in my mind.

I know what you are thinking: how can this be true? How can you be so happy, what about the days when you are feeling blue?

What about the days when you are sad, really frustrated, or really mad?

Well that's easy! I will tell you what I do; I will tell you what I tell myself to stop feeling blue.

I say to myself, "Bree, not today! You will NOT be sad! It will NOT happen,

"You will not walk with your head held down! You will raise it to the sky. You will stand up straight with your head held high!"

Whatever it is that is making me sad, this feeling that I have will surely pass.

Sadness will not stay. It might last for a little while, and then it must go on its way.

"I am Happy! I am Happy!" I say it with all my might, I tell myself this everyday with my smile big and bright!

Listen, friend: You should tell yourself this, too! Tell yourself that you are happy on the days when you are feeling blue.

Tell yourself "I am Happy!" and say it all the time, and you will begin to feel great. You will feel just fine!

Being happy is a great way to be. Tell yourself everyday, "I am Happy!" and you will feel just like me!

Made in the USA
Columbia, SC
13 September 2019